ERKIN VOHIDOV

Mukhsina Joraboyeva

Erkin Vohidov

by: Mukhsina Joraboyeva

Edition: February '2024

Publisher:

Taemeer Publications LLC (Michigan, USA / Hyderabad, India)

ISBN 978-93-5872-386-1

Book	:	Erkin Vohidov
Author	:	Mukhsina Joraboyeva
Publisher	:	Taemeer Publications
Year	:	'2024
Pages	:	30
Title Design	:	*Taemeer Web Design*

(He was born in 1936)

People's poet of Uzbekistan, a unique talent ***Erkin Vahidov*** is the shining star of our poetry. At the same time.He is a well-known Free Society in Vohidov District, intellectuals of 1936.

He was born in his family on December 28. Farg secondary school in the region with a gold medal, Tashkent State University (now UzMU) faculty of Uzbek philology with honors diploma graduated with <Young Guard> and in the name of Gafur Gu ulam He worked in literary and art publishing houses. Youth magazine In 1983, he became the editor-in-chief of Eastern with the state award of Uzbekistan for the collection of "coast". Awarded. The poet was awarded the Hero of Uzbekistan in 1999 was awarded the title Erkin Vahidov created in various genres of literature,he grew from work to work. In the creative growth of the poet, his people learning the life and skills of teachers is important got. Erkin Vahidov's creative learning from teachers,mainly in two ways: first, from his youth starting with Navoi, Fuzuli, Pushkin, Yesenin, H. Olimjon,After carefully reading the works of many great poets like Gayraty,learned That is why he, for example, Hamid Olimjon about: <I call him a teacher. It's the first time you read me led to the magic bouquet in absentiaverses poured into my young heart like a waterfall, am happy and the poet who taught me the art of singing joy,he wrote. Second, Erkin Vahidov's work Schiller, continued I. Abu Goethe, Ali A. Ibn Pushkin, Sino, S. Hafiz Yesenin, Shirozi, A. Blok, M. Bedil Svetlov, Friedrich A. Tvardovsky, Silva Kaputikyan, A. Malishko, Rasul Translation of several works of poets like Hamzatov Sergey Yesenin <Iran

did Especially L. Goethe's <Faust>,skillfully translated Taronalari's works into Uzbek. That's it in the process, it was influenced by the works of poets,many of them learned Erkin Vahidov entered literature in the 60s of the 20th century came His unique talent is primarily as a poet.It is clearly manifested in the innovations introduced into the Uzbek she riyat will be It is known that in the period when E. Vahidov entered literature High social pathos is the leader in poetry. of a person feelings were not allowed to be described properly. Free Vahidov broke this non-aesthetic belief and made poetry human to turn into an expression of feelings, with his life focus on strengthening the connection, giving artistic polish to the work turned He created great examples of real lyrics actively fought to improve the level of our poetry.Erkin Vahidov's early poems showed artistic skills,paid special attention to the quality of the work and very good results achieved This includes the poet's "Morning Breath" (1961), "Mind and Heart".(1963), <My Star> (1964) such early collections

full satisfaction can be obtained in the example. Because it is Most of the poems included in the collections are soft and charming are examples of lovely lyrics with a civic feel to them it blows. The poet glorifies true humanity in society.He was the creator of all material and spiritual wealth about human feelings and moods through the medium of speech art observes. The fate of society is in the hands of man sincerely expresses:

On a fixed planet, you are Human, you are Human,

Be a king, be a sultan

<Human>

Erkin Vahidov in his poetry, man, work, country,youth, friendship with sincerity in its strings, and beauty and purity, unique honesty, sweet eternal and correctness, smooth current love, sings the themes in style. devotion, lyrics In the poem"Beauty" not only the world of work, but also For example, changes the person himself; makes you beautiful and handsome,The idea is mastery represented by:

Everything is in one place,

The world was created without sight.

Polish the world to give

The universe was created by man. obido aids

Since then, people have been constantly researching

I'm still sweating over this place

1 sbiomoi aelsilon as he beautifies the earth

He will be beautiful, he is also human.

Erkin Vahidov the colorful topics of our time finger weight comfort in lighting, light weight he uses his opportunities with equal skill Indeed, Erkin Vahidov in the 60s: <O critic, you do

not underestimate the ghazal as old, love is also from Adam bold aesthetic point of view the rest is like human blood,had raised. At the same time, the poet is the spirit of the new age expression in works of aruz weight, including ghazals proved possible in practice.Damn AL From the poet's beautiful ghazals, epics and odes"Department of Youth" (1969) by Erkin Vahidov

Aruz has mastered the intricacies of weight, new age skillful in expressing his ideas from the traditional ghazal form demonstrated that it can be used. Erkin Vahidov's <Lola sayli>, <My youth, come>, <May all joy be yours>Many poems such as <Shirin>, <Have a prosperous home with a friend>are perfect, beautiful examples of the ghazal genre. Them the subjects drawn by the pen are of a high standard, very pleasant illuminated. Therefore, the verses in these ghazals are different It is strongly connected and creates a whole life picture creates a complete poetic-goyaic content. <With a friend In the ghazal of the prosperous house, the poet uses various visual means, the people creating wise verses at the level of proverbs and aphorisms Read his poetic conclusions about friendship

instills into the general spirit:

Have a prosperous home with a friend, even if it is a ruin,

If a friend does not take a step, the house is ruined.

Look for a friend, find a friend in the world, there are only a few hundred thousand friends,

Even if there are many enemies, it is only one.

The language of Erkin Vahidov's ghazals is free of artificial silence

Poet's verses flow very naturally and smoothly. That's why Almost all of Erkin Vahidov's ghazals are composed by composers and it is set to tune and sung by hafiz.Social in Erkin Vahidov's poetry of the 70s and 80s motivations increased. This feature is the poet's <Nido> (1965),<Today's youth> (1974), <Living planets> (1978), <Eastern coast> (1981), <Bedarlik> (1985), <Love"Zangori" included in collections such as

"Sadokatnoma" (1986).points>, <We are working>, <Benefit philosophy>, <Forget.It is evident in his poems such as "Song" and "Iron Geniuses".Thrown away. The poet social phenomena and social motives

in expressing the material and spiritual life of the Uzbek people refers to the fields. The historical past of the Uzbek people.In particular, he paints realistic scenes from the current lifestyle.

A vivid reflection of the national characteristics and national values of the people makes Especially the hard work of the Uzbek people.Humanity, patriotism, charity, kindness.I am fascinated by such wonderful qualities as consistency and tolerance describes as At the same time, the people's happiness joys, pains, anxieties, dreams and reflects his desires in a very impressive and attractive way.

Erkin Vahidov is a hard-working Uzbek in his poem <Uzbegim>by creating his nation/image, he has the right to the dignity of Uzbeks raised high. The rich and ancient history of Uzbek Poeticly asserting that they are a nation, he came to the following conclusion:

Your history is over, my people

a thousand Firdavisiy are needed,

Because you struble once

A thousand epics, Uzbegim

Poet Erkin Vahidov, rich history of the Uzbek people, national another nation when describing its values and wonderful qualities and does not discriminate against nations at all. He is a truly international artist as this important and sensitive topic is always the friendship of peoples approach from the point of view. Even when he wrote about the Russian people(Dawn of Great Life>), when he sang about the peoples of the Caucasus also (near the statue of Fuzuli>, <Azganush>), in Central Asia even when the poetic scenes from the life of the brothers ended (Tajik to my brother>, <Abay>, <to Kazakh refugees>), even abroad even when he penned his subject (<from the Canadian series>) Free

Vahidov has a sincere respect for foreign peoples illuminates based on Through this friendship, brotherhood, friendship and sincerely expresses feelings of friendship.The masses of our time in the poetry of Erkin Vahidov various issues of interest and concern,Various topics take the main place and they are life reflecting in a simple and fluent language with good intentions in accordance with the truth will be delivered. In one of his poems, Erkin Vahidov is a poet himself observations: <The world says: never my mother tongue died>, - concludes. The poet's works are instructive in life by describing aspects, bright principles, positive situations at the same time, it reveals negative aspects and various vices. Poet:My lord has two strings: one is happy, one is sad. That's my verse There are two lines: one is dilkhush, the other is dilhun>, he wrote this is what he meant. Indeed, the poet of our time.He sings proudly of our achievements as his eyes and ears the pains and sufferings of the living period with sadness shows.Erkin Vahidov mentions ancient national traditions in some of his poems worries about the erosion of values and stop it raises the question of putting.

The poet's <Political lesson or Bek Bekov's strange adventure> in the subject poem Bek Bekov, the head of the senior administration, is described one day not in a company car from the office to home, returns on foot. On the way, he encountered various strange adventures will come. As a result, his eyes are opened and he realizes his mistakes. In fact, it is Bek Bekov walking home of all kinds of suspicions and rumors in the neighborhood where he lives cause it to spread. Someone: He left if he guesses that, someone else: <There was a bite or something yes panic something to see. Yes, to the salty head that has fallen, he combs. And Shokirvoy, the tea shop owner, will definitely be there for him humble, simple, says words and gives <advice>. Actually, Beck an honest, impartial person. He has been busy all his life was He left for work early and came back late. <Meeting, election, speech, the end... From morning to evening. He never lived for himself never>>. In the end, Bek Bekov lives for business he realizes that he has become distant from the people of the neighborhood and from that will deeply regret:

Unripe head!

He will carry your coffin

After all, the neighborhood!

If there is a wedding, ask someone

Have you entered?

With a belt at the bottom

The world has seen, the mind is broad,

My glorious father

Don't think so, say

The minister is a man

It seems that in the work, the poet is in the character of some leaders scrutinizing subtle defects at an invisible level Ilgab has skillfully described them. From this life neighborhood learning; He put forward the idea of always being with the country, sharing both the joys and worries of the people. There is also the fact that the work glorifies our national values and promotes our traditions. Achievement is not stated in vain: on the contrary, to the general spirit of the work skillfully absorbed In the works of Erkin Vahidov, there is never a social conflict not overlooked. The poet rebuilds society and he also wrote bright poems about independence Erkin Vahidov's country, your caravan that set off on a long journey feelings, faith of the lyrical hero in a Bors poem. Hatred and anger towards evil terrorists is a national refreshment in her dress, she is clearly expressed in a beautiful way. Poet to glorify the period of independence and make it the apple of an eye with the idea of preserving the motherland and loyalty to the people sings tightly tied. Sincerity, honesty in the poem and lyrical sophistication swells:

I've seen good and bad days in this world,

I don't have a problem, it's okay, I'm old.

I am still a soldier of yours, my motherland,

May the arrow shot in your direction hit me...

You are the dawn, Motherland, in the sky of my heart

In the harmony of your free ancestors,

Mehring is in the faith of generations

Let the arrow shot at this faith hit me.

Thus, the main place in the work of Erkin Vahidov is the present dedicated to the portrayal of topical, social topics of the time deep, serious, thoughtful poems occupy. From this besides, based on a funny story or a comic situation in the poet's writing created cheerful, cheerful, full of sincere humor there are also poems. Wise village anecdotes of the poet included in the series <Village of Matmusa, <Matmusa hat, <Matmusa's plate>, <Matmusa's .charxpalagi, <Matmusa's tandirid, <Matmusa's marriage. <Curious Matmusa>, <Matmusa is an artist", Like <Matmusa's teacher>, <Matmusa wearing a tandoor> happy poems were liked by the readers. These poems along with giving students a good mood, them it also serves to educate in the spirit of goodness. Erkin Vahidov on various topics of the present time written comic poems are also important educational and aesthetic has value. Poet <Make a meeting>, Philosophy of interest> <don't touch me, <It's in my head>, <Advice>, <Hair song >He was present in his comic poems such as <Kochamen>laughs at all kinds of vices. Erkin Vahidov in his comic-humorous works <from the story expresses the output contribution in a very clear and concise manner,In one poem: <Don't make your hands skilled in work, make your tongue a master in speech,sarcastically, in another work: < From you and from me this>, <He washes his hands, my friend, If there is no need for a nephew, uncle(Benefit too, my

friend>,philosophy).In short, Erkin Vahidov is a diverse genre of poetry refers to the forms and every time it is new creates samples. The poet is concerned with the fate of the nation and the people both in his serious poems and in his humorous not by dry description of events, but rather the idea of the work artistic embodiment, simple and figurative, concise and profound goes the way of creating bytes and makes serious progress Poet's works are easy to digest. Of this the main reason is that the author is alive from the riches of language new-new, effectively using various visual media similes, great similes, vivid expressions, simple, but serhikmat creates verses.The poet's poem " If Uzbek people don’t read Navoiy...>". It is written with a bold, deep meaning there is wisdom. This big meaning in the work is a folk word and skillfully revealed with the help of expressions. Navoi reading and studying his works and widely promoting them among the people the great spiritual and educational importance of reaching with passion expressed as:

If Uzbek people do not read Navoi,

Struggling time that's what this is.

If he plays and laughs without enlightenment,

This is what happened during morning.

If Uzbek people do not read Navoi,

That's what he was deceived about.

If the fool is dear, and the scholar is despised,

That is what Paytava is a turban.

Erkin Vahidov's few works are abstract, silent and The riddle does not use verses. Deeply meaningful expresses thoughts in a simple, concise and figurative way. Everyone is a poet time uses words and phrases sparingly, without wasting too much, and in the end sparingly. That's why it's free Vahidov's poetry is the first element of a literary work very clear and fluent, concise and beautiful language,It is different from the work of many other poets due to its compactness and imagery makes, stands out. Two volumes by Erkin Vahidov <Election)> works (<Love> and <Loyalty)complete satisfaction when reading it, Erkin Vahidov, along with writing wonderful lyric poems,<Dawn of a Great Life> (1960), <Fountain of Dreams>, <Shout> (1964).<An epic written in a palace> (1966), <The dwelling of the sun> (1970).<Charog'bon> (1971), <Bakhmab> (1974), <Rebellion of Spirits (1979)He also created various epics. These epics most of them - both in terms of content and artistic skills also strong and handsome. They have various topics that are deep and readable reflected as The epic <Nido> is dedicated to the theme of war, beginning the hero is a twenty-year-old man, this is life and death a generalization of the new generation that came of age after the war is an image. The work is with the grassy cry of this lyrical hero starts The epic <Nido> is written in a light style with juicy language. It has many touching and catchy lyrical passages. Erkin Vahidov's epic "Rebellion of Spirits" - ideological- an artistic masterpiece. The poet has his national independence and human being with mastery of political ideas about the essence of freedom expressed. The story takes place in India.The life and tragic fate of the revolutionary Indian poet Nazrul Islam was taken as the basis for the subject of the epic. story and main character "Rebellion of Spirits" epic as a special treasure of wisdom.It contains many auspicious verses that never get old So, Erkin Vahidov's achievements in epic writing and his contribution to this genre are huge.

Erkin Vahidov is also known as a talented playwright.His first stage work is called "The Second March"is a product of the 1960s. Free tragicomedy Vahidov's most famous stage work <The Golden Wall (1970)is a comedy. The first work is the Uzbek State named after Hamza in the Academic Drama

Theater (now the National Academic Theater)successfully staged for many years.The audience took a strong place in the theater repertoire received applause. <Golden Wall> in 2001 It was also staged in a prestigious theater of Pakistan and the audience liked it. The comedy <Golden Wall> is deep in content artistically perfect as it is. He is a comedy fully meets the requirements of the genre. From the beginning of the work laughs (humor) until the end. After all, it's funny.A funny story with substance and conflicts skillfully is displayed. Playwright. Lust for wealth in comedy and over the desire to gain wealth by harsh means laughs Disgraceful and impure persons. That's it based on the idea of working honestly and living honestly absorbs.The main characters in the work, in particular, the main character Mo'min has a completely comic character. This image is a great skill created with A believer is worthy of his name carefree simple, sincere and honest person. When he found a cocoon full of gold,loses his mood, falls into various situations: sometimes he is happy sometimes suffering and finally to the point of going crazy will go. Playwright Mo'min and people around him showing bright and vivid scenes from his life. of comedy expressed its ideological content in an interesting and effective way. In this it is sarcasm, teasing, jokes, jokes, puns and other means of laughter, as well as psychoanalysis skillfully used. The language of the work as well as the subject and images it is also created at a high level, beautiful and elegant"Tragedy of Istanbul" (1985) in Erkin Vahidov's works is poetic drama plays an important role. Purity and impurity in the work.Crookedness with straightness, hypocrisy with honesty, justice with injustice, the tension between sincerity and fakeness struggle is vividly reflected. The subject of the work is vital and interesting built on the basis of conflict and extremely attractive and impressive created. There are mainly three characters in the drama "Istanbul Tragedy": the chairman Jalal, his wife Saodat and his brother Iskandar are among them all three are shown in accordance with the reality of life and the work the idea of these characters' activities, actions,skillfully inserted into his dialogues and monologues. After many years of separation of this hero the meeting is the climax of the drama plot and The work is the richest and most impressive in the dramatic situations as its pages shake the reader's heart. Because it is the reality of life in a meeting, the fate of confused destinies.The root causes of terrible events with Shakespearean skill revealed. Jalal says about this meeting:

I didn't sleep a moment last night

My whole life flashed before my eyes one by one,

Iskandar's pain suffered for many years

Today I forgave my heart overnight.

I am not here with my dead brother,

I met a dead conscience.

Playwright describe the situation, Jalal's last mental from this meeting forgery through remembering his past the glory of vices like eye make-up, ambition represents honestly the impact it had on fate Jalal's pity expressed as: his own language is very clear and effective.

I am a man who has lived my life, now

Should the children have a false inheritance from me?

I have to say something while I'm alive,

At least I should rest in peace...

“Pretense and forgery in the tragedy of Istanbul” drama along with fate, the tragedy of patriotism is revealed.When Iskandal met his brother Jalal abroad, first of all: <A handful of soil from the motherland didn't you bring it?> - he asks. And Jalal: it grew in the soil there are raisins>, - he gives him a raisin. Alexander: "Thank you ,Thank you, I felt like I could breathe my country," he said. Iskandar: I wish I could die in your arms again.I would leave the world unscathed. As if he was sleeping in his mother's arms like a child, I would be pampered on the ground>, - he moaned does, cries.By showing the bitter fate of the playwright Alexander.How sacred is the feeling of Motherland that it is priceless, comparing it to nothing else very impressively showed that it will not happen. Thus,the ideas of love for the Motherland masterfully applied to the subject of the work imbibed<Istanbul Tragedy> is also artistically mature. Drama Philosophical with deep meaning, corresponding to the reality of life a deep one who has risen to the level of generalizations and wisdom overflowing with meaningful thoughts. From the language of Happiness at the end of the drama Good human qualities in the words about Alexander greatness noted:

Now I know that the truth is a high mountain,

You can turn a blind eye to it, you can look away

But it is impossible to bury with soil,

Now my last word to you: Go back to your country,

The past is over, now is the rest of my life

Let's live honestly and cleanly, not with lies

This poetic drama is meticulous in language, rhyme and weight, made in the norm. However, there are some flaws in the work

Negative aspects of Jalal's chairmanship, complex problems if reflected more widely and deeply, the reality of the time is more would have been revealed more clearly. There is insufficient evidence in the work therefore, some event with weak persuasive power and A description of the situation is found. The name of the drama is its content not very suitable. Because the tragedy is not in Istanbul, but somewhere else happened at the place. The brothers met in Istanbul before they only remembered the tragedies that happened. On the whole <Tragedy of Istanbul> is the achievement of our dramaturgy.It should be noted that Erkin Vahidov's work is Uzbek in the 20th century as one of the greatest and most valuable achievements of literature.Since the 60s, literary criticism and literature-has been attracting the attention of scholars.In literary studies, including O. Sharafiddinov L. Qayumov, U. Normatov, I. Gafurov, N. Khudoyberganov. Erkin Vahidov in the scientific works of N. Shukurov and others The main features of his work have been analyzed quite extensively. This if the important scientific research work is continued further, Erkin Vahidov's multi-faceted and effective creativity is great.If monographs were created, it would be the same.So, Erkin Vahidov, the owner of natural talent, is the roof a national poet in a sense. Uzbek poetry of the 20th century was written by this poet cannot be imagined without creativity. The work of the poet is many countries honored with awards and titles. E. Vahidov in 1987<People's poet of Uzbekistan>, "Hero of Uzbekistan" in 1999 received titles. 1997 <Great services for> awarded with the order.

www.ingramcontent.com/pod-product-compliance
Lightning Source LLC
LaVergne TN
LVHW010422070526
838199LV00064B/5389

* 9 7 8 9 3 5 8 7 2 3 8 6 1 *